9780603057847
AF471015

For T.S.W.
Crow Indian
Chief

Dean's Gold Star Book of

written & illustrated

by

Janet & Anne Grahame Johnstone

603 05784 5

Pipes

There were originally many tribes of Indians.

The warrior opposite is a Head Chief of the MANDAN tribe, who lived along the upper Missouri river.

The chief's war bonnet is made of raven's feathers trimmed with dyed horse hair, feathers and ermine tails. His buckskin shirt has beaded decoration and is trimmed with ermine tails, horse hair and scalp locks from the heads of his enemies.

He holds a ceremonial peace pipe in his hand. The ceremonial pipes were used in religious ceremonies. Beautifully decorated, the pipes had wooden or bamboo stems; the bowls were sometimes stone and marvellously carved.

The warrior's nine-foot lance was used in war and hunting. The war clubs had leather-covered stones at the head or heavy wooden heads. They too were decorated with beads and leather fringes.

The tomahawk or war axe was originally stone, but later had a metal blade.

This is a camp of the SHOSHONI tribe. The tents on the higher ground house the Indians on lookout for the enemies of their tribe.

In the foreground women are scraping and preparing hides for tents (called tipis) and clothes.

Tipis were made of buffalo hides sewn together and stretched round a tripod of long poles. The poles were tied together at the top, with a hole left for the smoke to get out.

The tipi was warm in winter and cool in summer, and strong enough to stand up in a gale. It was not difficult to put up the tipi.

Strict politeness was important among the Indians, and it was bad manners to enter a tipi uninvited or to walk between another guest and the fire. Young men and children remained silent unless invited to speak, and everyone left at a signal from their host.

feather head dress
medicine bag
buckskin shirt
breech clout
buckskin leggings
buffalo cloak
moccasins

The Indians lived by fishing and hunting for food and fine animal skins. They moved to the best grounds at suitable times of the year.

Here, on a hot summer evening, young men of the CHIPPEWA tribe, in their canoes near Lake Superior, are scooping quantities of fish out of the shallow water.

An Indian mother of the SIOUX tribe plays with her little baby.

Babies were very much loved and almost never smacked. When a few weeks old they were laced into cradle boards for most of the day. The cradle board had a soft skin pouch inside it and a padded frame at the top to protect the baby's face.

Little toys and charms dangled in front for the baby to play with.

Indian women wore soft buckskin dresses, leggings and moccasins. These were decorated with fringes, hair and beads.

Many of the Indian men and women had very long hair of which they were extremely proud. The CROW Indian braves' hair was as much as nine or ten feet long. Their hairbrushes were made from the stiff-haired tail of the porcupine, stitched round a stout stick and beaded.

Among the tools used by Indian women the awl was used to pierce holes in the hides, to make sewing clothes, tipis and harness easier.

The burden strap had goods or baggage tied to it and was then carried on a woman's back.

The bone hide-scraper was used to scrape the hair and fat off new skins, which were then prepared for wearing.

The basket was woven from rushes, grasses, bark or leaves. Grain or clothes or household things were kept in it.

The babies' little charm holders were kept for luck for the rest of their lives.

Before the Spaniards first brought horses to America, the Indians used their women and strong dogs to carry their baggage, while the men hunted and protected the tribe from attack.

They seldom marched more than six miles a day. With the coming of horses it was possible to travel fifteen to thirty miles a day.

The dogs and horses were harnessed to a travois. The travois was two long poles lashed crosswise near the tips and fastened to the horse's harness. There was a platform at the back on which women or children or baggage sat. Sometimes a big wicker basket or cage with small children safely enclosed was tied to the platform.

The dogs pulled smaller travois; occasionally there were dog fights and the baggage was upset. The dogs were sometimes crossed with wild wolves, and they were strong, hardy creatures with keen scent and a swift pace for hunting.

Two Indian boys play with a toy bow and spear. The boys learned to ride and shoot as soon as they could walk. Their fathers praised their successes and called friends and family to admire their skill.

Good manners, generosity and a manly way of behaving was encouraged by parents.

The Indians thought it a disgrace and shaming to be criticised or gossiped about.

Indian boys' playthings were usually miniature weapons. Wooden tomahawks and clubs were made especially for them, and blunt arrows. They also had toy horses and warrior dolls.

The flute is a courting flute or love flute. It was played in the evening or at night to please the Indian girls.

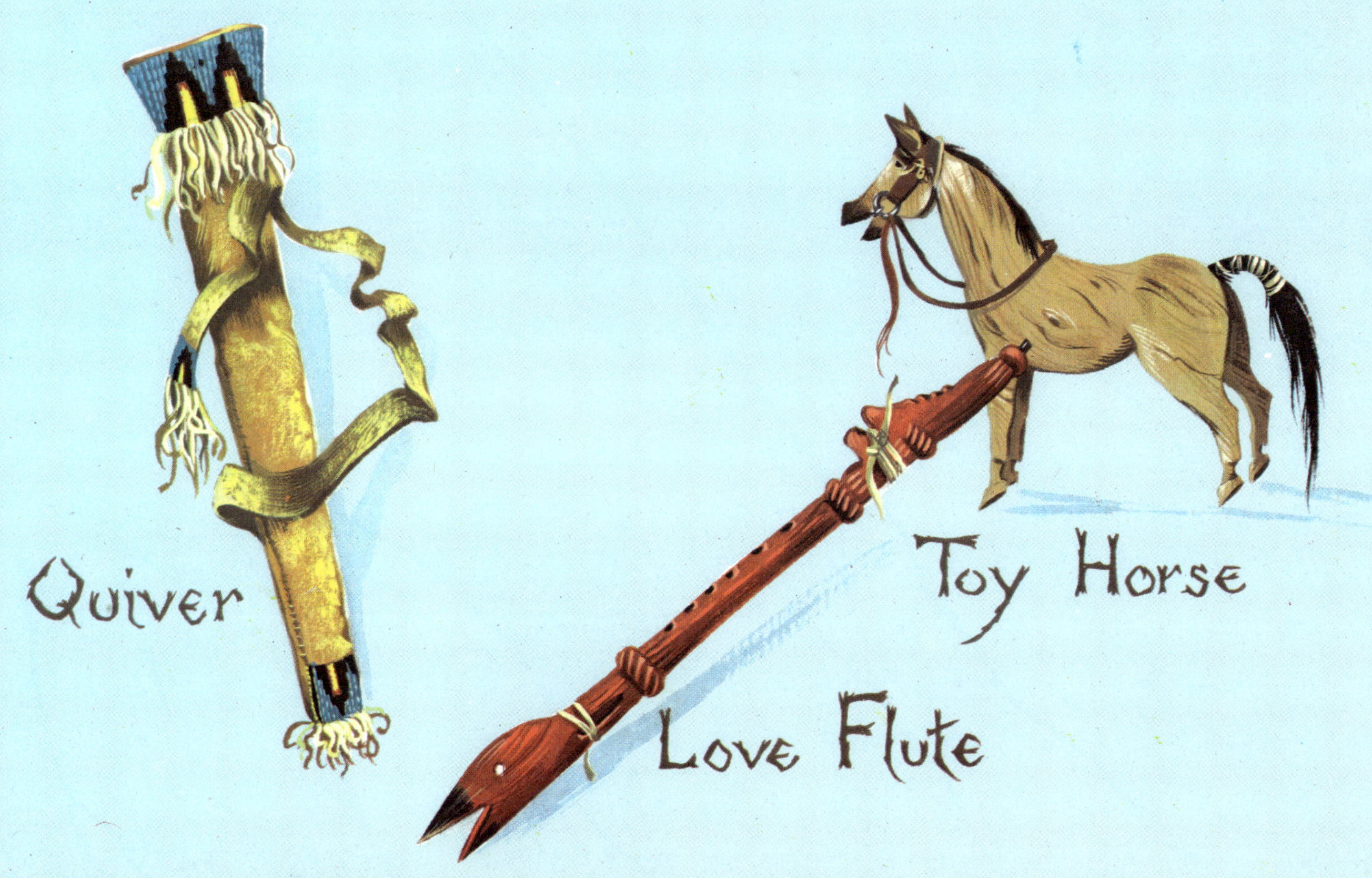

Little girls helped their mothers by looking after their baby brothers or sisters and keeping them amused.

This cradle board is different from the one on the previous page. It comes from the ARAPAHO tribe.

Girls learned to sew, prepare hides and cook. Sometimes the boys would hunt for things for them to cook. Toy tipis were used for playing 'houses'.

Dolls

Children had many games and boys and girls were all expert swimmers, crossing the fastest and roughest rivers.

The dolls have come from many different tribes. There were baby dolls, and dolls dressed like grown-up men and women.

Some dolls were used in dances and religious ceremonies, where they represented gods or spirits.

This MANDAN tribe Buffalo Dance took place before a buffalo hunt.

It was led by two great warriors wearing buffalo heads that had been specially prepared. The men stamped and shuffled round a fire, while the other braves milled round them imitating stampeding buffalo.

Buffalo provided for nearly all the Indians' needs: meat for food, fresh or dried in the sun; bone and horn for weapons and tools, and fat for preserving leather.

The buffalo roamed the vast prairies, sometimes in enormous herds of thousands, sometimes a few dozen. They were very large, strong, short-sighted and bad-tempered. Before they had horses, the Indians found them more difficult to hunt.

With horses the Indians would stalk a herd, then round them up into a tight group. With shouts and yells they would gallop round and round until the buffalo were running in a small circle or mill.

The bravest warriors on the boldest horses would ride into the midst of the charging buffalo to spear the best. Men and horses were often killed on buffalo hunts, which were very dangerous.

The Medicine or Mystery Man was the Indians' doctor. Some medicine men had great skill in healing and all relied on songs, dances and awesome costumes to inspire respect.

This BLACKFOOT tribe medicine man wears the skin of a great bear of an unusual yellow colour. Many of the animal, bird and reptile skins that dangled from him had something strange about them; odd colouring or extra legs, heads or toes. This was thought to be powerful 'medicine'.

The medicine man danced or crept round his patient, giving strange cries and yelps and startling jumps. He often used rattles, drums or dolls in his ceremonies.

Every Indian from the age of about eleven had his own medicine bag. This was usually the skin of an animal, sometimes small like a mouse or mole, sometimes bigger like a fox. The medicine bag was usually stuffed with dry grass and decorated. It was a sacred charm. To the Indian it was a sacred charm which guarded his life and health, and he prayed and sacrificed to it all his life.

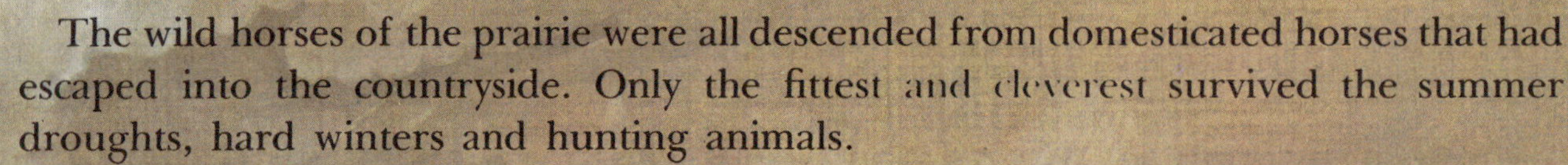

The wild horses of the prairie were all descended from domesticated horses that had escaped into the countryside. Only the fittest and cleverest survived the summer droughts, hard winters and hunting animals.

The Indians valued their horses above everything and counted their riches in horses. From them they gained speed, to hunt and fight, strength, to move their tribe and baggage, and mobility. They used the stallions as war horses and the mares for breeding and to carry baggage.

Travellers to America found many of the Indian horses both beautiful and fast, and very tough. The best horses were never caught; they nearly always escaped. The

Indians considered the horse the most cunning and difficult animal to hunt.

The stallions who commanded the herds were watchful and cunning. They could see and hear over great distances. As a rule only the stragglers of the herd were caught.

Using snow shoes made of supple wicker and thongs of sinew, a party of Indians hunt buffalo in the snow.

Some are using flat sleds pulled by dogs.

They drive the buffalo into deep snow drifts from which it is difficult to escape. Here they spear the buffalo to provide much needed winter food, without which their tribe would perish.